BUILDING HOMES

Graham Rickard

Houses and Homes

Building Homes
Castles and Mansions
Homes in Cold Places
Homes in Hot Places
Homes in Space
Homes in the Future
Homes on Water
Mobile Homes

All words printed in
bold are explained in
the glossary on page 30

Cover illustration: Building apartments on a
construction site in Bavaria.

Editor: Sarah Doughty

Designer: Sally Boothroyd

First published in 1988 by
Wayland (Publishers) Ltd
61 Western Road, Hove,
East Sussex BN3 1JD, England

© 1988 Wayland (Publishers) Ltd

British Library Cataloguing in Publication Data
Rickard, Graham
Building Homes — (Houses and homes)
1. Dwellings — Juvenile literature
I. Title II. Series
643 TX303
ISBN 1-85210-186-5

Typeset by Oliver Dawkins, Burgess Hill, West Sussex
Printed in Italy by G. Canale & C.S.p.A., Turin
Bound in Belgium by Casterman S.A., Tournai

Contents

What is a home?

In spite of the advances which humans have made during thousands of years of progress, we still have the same two basic needs as most other creatures — food and shelter. For survival and comfort people have always needed homes to protect them from the weather, wild animals and their enemies.

Our homes are places where we feel safe to eat, sleep, relax, raise children and keep our belongings, in comfort and in private.

The first human shelters were prehistoric caves, or simple huts of stones and branches. Over the centuries, building skills have made great progress. New materials and building techniques make today's homes more efficient and comfortable than ever before.

Throughout the world, people live in many different types of homes. These vary according to the local climate, the available building materials and the needs and customs of the people who live in the different parts of the world.

Left *Homes in north Sydney, Australia.*

Right *Some people live in unusual homes such as these floating homes in Vancouver, Canada.*

Below *Because of the high cost of land in cities, many people around the world live in tower blocks similar to these in West Berlin.*

Wherever they live, people have always found ways of using local materials to build a safe home for themselves and their families. Local conditions influence the homes they build, so while some people live underground others live high up in skyscraper blocks, or on the water in floating homes.

All these homes may look very different, but they all provide the same basic human needs of shelter, safety and comfort.

Building with wood

Wood is the oldest and easiest to use of all the world's building materials. It is light, strong and easy to cut and shape with simple tools. It can be joined with joints, glue, nails, screws, ropes or modern metal fasteners.

Wood looks attractive, **insulates** well against heat and cold, and will last a very long time if properly cared for. Wood for building is called timber, and can be used to make floors, walls and roofs, as well as window frames, doors and many other parts of a house. It can be used in more ways than any other building material.

All timber is divided into two types: hard woods, from leaf-shedding trees, such as oak; and soft woods, from evergreen conifer trees. Hard woods are usually heavier and longer lasting. They are often used for the outer parts of a building which are exposed to the weather. The cheaper soft woods can safely be used for any inner parts, that are protected by the walls and roof.

One method of building with wood is to use whole tree trunks or branches laid on top of each other, and held in place with upright posts. This method wastes a lot of timber.

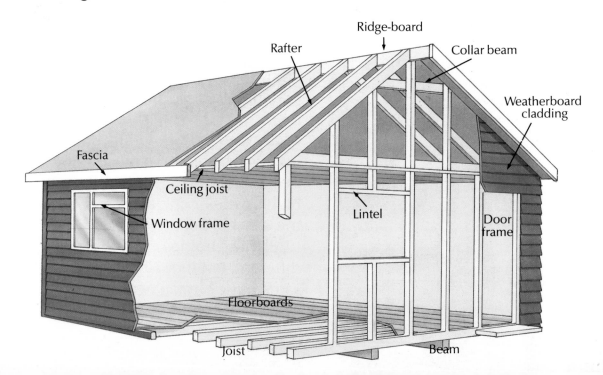

Timber can be saved by sawing the trunks into sections and planks for different uses. Larger timbers are used to build the frame of the house, which is then covered with horizontal 'weatherboard' **cladding**. This traditional way of building timber houses is still used in many countries which have large forests, such as Sweden and the USA.

To make large, strong sheets for floors and walls, strips or chips of wood can be pressed into shape with glue. Modern wood-based products include plywood, chipboard and fibreboard.

Another important product of wood, paper, is used to make elegant houses in Japan.

Above *A building site in California, USA where the basic material used for building is wood.*

Left *Diagram showing the parts of a house that are built with wood.*

Right *This wooden house is typical of homes in the southern states of the USA.*

Using plant and animal materials

Trees provide not only timber from their trunks, but also branches, twigs, leaves and bark, which can all be used for building houses. Wattle walls are made by weaving twigs around upright poles set in the ground. This method is often used to build houses in Thailand and parts of Africa. The wattle can be covered in a mixture of mud and cow dung called **wattle and daub**, to make the walls more weatherproof.

Grass, turf, moss, heather and reeds are all widely used wherever they grow in large quantities. These plant materials are especially useful for making watertight roofs. Overlapping bundles of reeds or straw, held in place with split twigs, are used to make thatched roofs.

In Ireland and Scandinavia, special spades are used to cut long strips of turf, which are sewn with grass to make a living roof that is warm and waterproof.

In Africa, some people build Kirdi shelters, with a roof of grass on wooden poles. This protects them from the blazing sun.

In the marshlands of southern Iraq, reeds grow up to 7 m long, and are used to make striking homes.

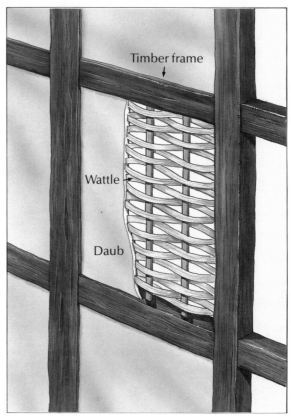

Timber frame

Wattle

Daub

Left *Mud is plastered over a framework of woven sticks to make this wattle and daub home in Kenya.*

Right *Long strips of woven cloth are sewn together to make Bedouin tents.*

Left *The structure of wattle and daub.*

Below *The Marsh Arabs build homes using giant reeds.*

Animals provide many useful building materials. Native North Americans make a cone-shaped framework of long poles, which is then covered with animal skins to complete their traditional tepee.

The hair from sheep, goats and camels can be woven into a fabric to make tents, such as those used by the nomadic Bedouin tribes.

In Mongolia and Iran, some people live in circular 'yurts', which are tents made by placing a covering of felt over a lattice frame. The felt is made by pressing animal hairs together. A yurt provides a strong home for a whole family.

Building with mud and clay

Above *Repairing the wall of an adobe house in New Mexico, USA. Clay is mixed with water and smoothed over the surface with a trowel. The walls dry hard in the sun.*

In many countries throughout the world, earth and clay have always been popular materials for building walls and floors. But earth is quickly washed away by heavy rain, and is most suitable for hot, dry climates.

African mud homes are made from soil mixed with water, which is then shaped by hand until the circular walls reach the right height. Small doors and windows are cut when the mud is still damp, and the thatched roof is added when the walls have hardened in the sun.

Arab builders use mud bricks to build thick walls, with tiny windows to keep out the sun's rays.

In some countries, such as Mexico, clay blocks are dried in the sun to make **adobe** walls. Liquid clay sticks the blocks together and gives the walls a smooth outer covering.

Mud or clay can be made stronger by mixing it with materials such as straw, animal hair or cow dung. In some parts of Europe, such as south-west England, **cob** walls are made from a mixture of clay, pebbles, sand and straw. Each layer is left to dry before the next is added. A sharp spade is used to cut the doors and windows. The walls are given a waterproof coating of tar or limewash.

In developing countries, where concrete and bricks are often too expensive, a new technique may provide the answer to people's housing needs. A simple hand press has been invented which uses a mixture of soil and cement (or lime) to produce strong, regular soil blocks. These can be used in the same way as bricks. Six people can produce 40 blocks an hour using this machine. The new blocks last up to 30 years, and have already been used to build new villages in Kenya, Nigeria and the Caribbean.

Below *This country cottage in south-west England has cob walls: a mixture of materials such as clay, straw and sand, covered with a waterproof coating.*

Above *The Brepak block-making machine is operated by hand to make building blocks from soil.*

Building with stone

Stone is the most hard-wearing of all building materials. Wherever there is a local supply, it has always been used to build solid, long-lasting houses. But stone is expensive because it is difficult to quarry (remove from the ground), cut and work with.

There are two types of building stone. **Ashlar** is cut and shaped into regular blocks, and can be used for a whole house or just to strengthen corners, or quoins, and areas surrounding the door and windows. **Rubble** buildings are made of rough, natural lumps of stone which may be laid in layers, or **courses**, or piled up to make a wall.

Stonework (and brickwork) is called masonry. The stonemason usually uses a **mortar** made from lime or cement and sand to stick the stones together.

Some stones are easier to use than others. Most limestones and sandstones are good for building with because they are easily shaped with a mason's hammer and chisel, but hard enough to stand up to rain and frost.

Marble can be finely carved into delicate shapes.

Granite is a very hard stone, and can only be used in large square

Left *A small quarry in Kenya where the men are using a variety of hand tools to remove lumps of stone from the ground. One quarrier is squaring off the stones and giving them a smooth finish.*

blocks, while flint is often split to show a shiny flat surface. This is a process called 'knapping.'

Slate is easily split into thin sheets, which are often used for roofing.

Slabs of natural stone make an attractive finish for modern tower blocks. A recent technique uses crushed stone mixed with cement to produce moulded building blocks. This is cheaper and easier to use than natural stone.

Even small fragments of stone can be used for attractive outer finishes. Small pebbles can be thrown against wet cement to produce the 'pebble-dash' wall finish.

Above *Slate quarrying in France. The slate quarrier taps the slate with a heavy tool, and the stone splits cleanly into thin sheets.*

Left *Knapped flint covers the lower half of the wall where the stone has been split to show a dark, shiny surface.*

13

Building with bricks

Bricks are regular-shaped blocks of clay, which are left to dry and then fired in a very hot kiln (like an oven). Bricks were first used thousands of years ago, when they were moulded by hand. Later, the use of rectangular wooden moulds made them more regular in size and shape. Hand-moulded bricks are still made in many countries including India and Malawi.

Modern brick **extrusion** machines squeeze out the clay in long strips, which are sliced to the right size with wire cutters. The standard modern brick measures 22. 7 cm × 11. 4 cm × 7. 5 cm — a size which fits the adult human hand comfortably.

It is easier to build with bricks than with stone, but the techniques are very similar. The bricks are laid in courses, with the vertical (upright) joints overlapping, to prevent weaknesses in the wall. The bricklayer uses mortar to stick the bricks together and removes the excess mortar with a trowel.

Brick walls can be built only a few courses at a time so that the wall does not lose its shape under the weight of the bricks while the mortar is still soft. The bricklayer often uses a **spirit level** and **plumbline** to make sure that the courses are even and the wall is vertical.

Right *A rectangular hand mould is being used by this builder in Mexico to make regular-shaped bricks.*

Bricks can be cut to size with a sharp blow from a trowel. Some bricks have a hollow, called a 'frog' in the top surface, which fills with mortar to give a better bond.

Bricks laid lengthways are called 'stretchers'. 'Headers' are laid end-on. 'Commons' are low-quality bricks for inner walls and facing bricks are used for outer walls.

Engineering bricks are strong enough to be used in the **foundations** and **footings** that support the whole house.

Perforated air-bricks (bricks made with tiny holes in them) allow air into the bricks and help to prevent them holding in too much water from the rain or damp.

Above *Freshly made bricks being stacked on to a wheel barrow at a brick factory in Brazil.*

Right *A builder uses a stretched piece of string to make sure that a course is perfectly even.*

Building with concrete

Concrete is a mixture of cement, sand, stones and water. The cement acts as a glue which sticks the stones together, and the sand fills in any spaces between the stones. Concrete sets rock hard, but while it is still wet it can be sprayed into shape or poured into moulds.

Because it is so strong, fairly small concrete sections can be used to support very large weights, and concrete is an ideal material for building skyscrapers and blocks of flats.

Reinforced (strengthened) concrete is even stronger, and is made by pouring the concrete around steel mesh or bars. If the bars are stretched until the concrete sets, this makes 'pre-stressed' concrete. Other materials, such as glass fibre or plastic are also used to make the concrete stronger.

On a building site, small amounts of concrete are mixed by hand, but larger amounts are delivered ready-mixed and poured or pumped from the lorry. Wood or metal **shuttering** is used to shape the concrete on site. When the concrete has set, the shuttering is removed and used for the next section of the building.

Sometimes the concrete sections are delivered ready-made from the factory, which saves time on the building site.

Concrete can also be made into blocks, which are much larger and much quicker to build with than bricks.

Lightweight blocks, which are good for insulating the house against loss of heat and outside noise, are made by bubbling air through the concrete in moulds. Ash and sand are often mixed in to make the blocks cheaper to produce. Concrete blocks are often used to build the inner walls of a house.

Above *Ready-mixed concrete being poured from a lorry into wooden shuttering.*

Left *A cement factory in Sicily.*

Right *The strength of concrete makes it an ideal material for building skyscrapers.*

Building with metal

Most houses use metal in the form of nails and screws, hinges, window-frames, wires and pipes, but it is only fairly recently that metal has been used as a material giving a house its structure.

Reinforced steel **joists** (RSJs) are built into some houses to support the weight over a door or window opening. But steel **girder construction** is usually only seen in modern 'high-rise' blocks of flats. For its weight, steel is a very strong material, and a steel framework acts as a skeleton that supports the weight of the whole building. Unlike most buildings, the walls do not have to support anything. They just fill in the gaps of the steel framework.

For added strength, the girders are made in an 'I'-section shape. They are bolted, **rivetted** or welded together to form the vertical and horizontal supports for each floor, which is usually made from concrete.

The outer 'curtain' walls, which act as a skin and protect the building, can be made of brick, glass, sheet metal, or any other material.

Using a crane to lift the heavy girders into position, each storey (floor) is built up in a series of box shapes. Sometimes the central crane tower is left in place to form the lift shaft for a large tower block.

Throughout the world, many poor people live just outside large cities in **shanty** towns. They have to build their homes from whatever they can find. They often use corrugated metal sheets as a cheap form of roofing. If a family is forced to move to another area, they may take their roof with them.

Left *A welder uses the heat from a gas torch to cut through a steel girder.*

Right *A steel girder framework acts as a skeleton to support the weight of a high-rise building.*

Below *A shanty town with corrugated iron roofs in a city suburb in Brazil.*

Preparing the site

In many parts of the world, people still build their own homes, helped by family and friends. They use traditional designs and are very skilled at using local materials. House building using modern building methods may require the skills of many different people.

The first job is to measure and survey the building site. The surveyor uses tape measures, **theodolites** and levels to produce a site plan, which shows the size and shape of the plot.

The **architect** works from the site plan and designs the house, and produces detailed drawings of every part of the building. These plans have to be checked by the local authority, who then give permission for work to go ahead.

Large earth-moving machines clear and level the site, and rough roads are laid so that it can be reached by the construction team.

Using surveying instruments, the site foreman supervises as the foundations of the walls are marked out with strings and wooden pegs. Mechanical excavators (digging machines) dig out the deep trenches for the foundations of the house. These foundations must be strong enough to stop the house sinking into the ground and cracking under its own weight.

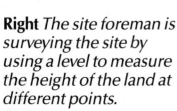

Right *The site foreman is surveying the site by using a level to measure the height of the land at different points.*

Liquid concrete is poured into the trenches, which sets to form a solid foundation. The floors of each room are dug out and partly filled with a **hard-core** of brick and stone rubble. This too is covered with a layer of concrete, or joists are laid to support a wooden floor.

On top of the foundations, bricklayers use strong engineering bricks to lay the underground footings for the outer walls. These are wider than the wall above, to spread the weight of the house over a larger area.

Above *Liquid concrete being poured into trenches to form a solid foundation.*

Right *Laying concrete joists to support the ground floor.*

Building the walls

In many developed countries, most modern houses are built of bricks. The bricklayer lays the corners of each wall and stretches a string line between them as a guide for laying each course of bricks in the wall.

Outside walls must be much thicker than the inner walls dividing the rooms, and are sometimes built with a gap, or cavity, in the middle. The outer 'skin' needs good quality bricks, while the inner wall can be made of concrete blocks or other material. For added strength, the two walls are joined with metal 'ties' and the cavity is sometimes filled with insulation material.

After the first few courses of bricks, the bricklayer puts in a layer of slate or tarred felt, called a damp-proof course (DPC). It stops the wall from soaking up the moisture in the ground. Polythene is laid under concrete floors for the same reason.

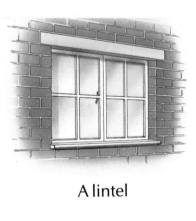

A lintel

A brickwork arch

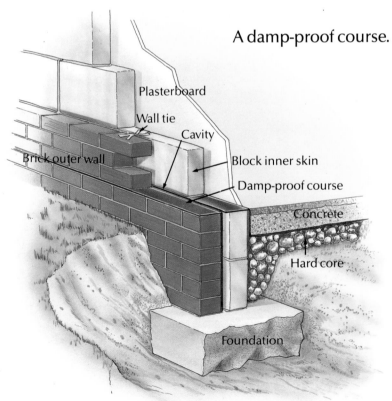

A damp-proof course.

Plasterboard

Wall tie

Cavity

Brick outer wall

Block inner skin

Damp-proof course

Concrete

Hard core

Foundation

The site carpenters fix the door and window frames in place in the gaps left by the bricklayers. Brick arches or concrete **lintels** are laid above each door or window opening to support the weight of the wall above.

Before the mortar sets too hard between the bricks, it is rubbed and 'pointed' with a small trowel to give a smooth and waterproof joint.

Timber frame houses need only a thin outer skin of brick to protect the wood, and the inside of the frame is covered with a thin layer of plasterboard.

Timber frames are usually delivered in ready-made sections. In Germany's modern factories, tree trunks are fed in at one end and complete houses come out at the other!

Above *Building a wall in south Tanzania using large hand-made bricks. The builder is using mud to hold the bricks together.*

Left *A bricklayer building a cavity wall with insulation on a steel-framed building.*

Building the roof

In most houses, the roof is the most difficult part to build. Flat roofs are suitable in dry climates, where they often provide extra living or storage space. In areas where there is more rain, roofs are usually sloping, or **pitched**, to allow water to run off easily into the gutters. Most roofs are built with overhanging **eaves** to protect the walls and may have vertical **gables**. Roofs are usually made up of a timber framework, covered with a waterproof material.

On top of the brick walls, the carpenter lays a wooden wall-plate: a piece of wood on which the horizontal joists are laid. These will support the upstairs ceilings.

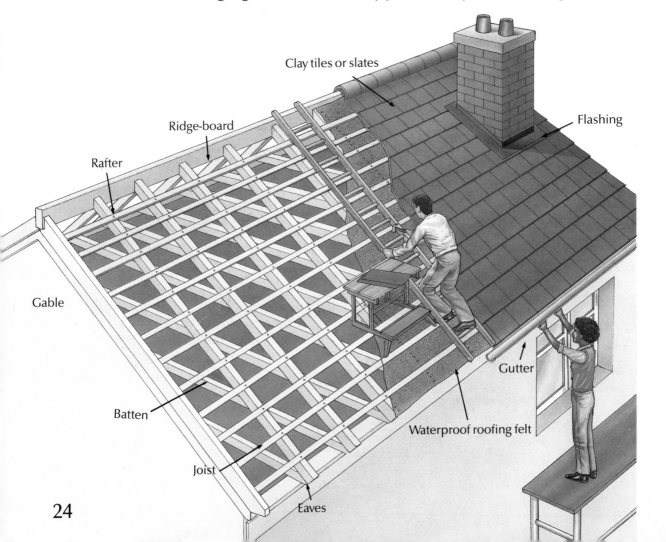

Clay tiles or slates

Flashing

Ridge-board

Rafter

Gable

Batten

Joist

Eaves

Gutter

Waterproof roofing felt

24

Right *The thatcher is fastening overlapping bundles of straw on to the roof timbers to make a thatched roof.*

Left *A tiler is fixing roof tiles to wooden battens while the gutters are put in place, underneath the eaves.*

The solid timbers that make the sloping **rafters** are cut to the right shape and length, and nailed into place. Each pair of rafters is joined at the top to the **ridge-board**, and at the bottom to the wall-plate. A horizontal **brace** connects each pair of rafters, to make an 'A'-shape. This gives the roof added strength.

The framework is then covered with overlapping layers of waterproof roofing-felt. Strips of wooden **batten** are nailed across the length of the roof. These support the final layer of cladding material, such as clay tiles, slates or thatch.

Strips of lead **flashing** are used for waterproof joints, wherever the roof meets a chimney or other obstacle.

Gutters and 'down pipes', usually made of plastic, are fixed all around the bottom of the roof. They carry water quickly away to the underground drains.

The spaces beneath the eaves and gable ends are protected from wind and rain by wood panels.

25

Light, heat and water

People need shelter. They also need heat to keep them warm and to cook food; water for drinking and washing; and light for the hours of darkness.

In modern houses throughout the world, clean water, light and warmth are available by turning a tap or clicking a switch. Mains supplies of water, electricity and gas, together with flush toilets and good sewage systems (these carry away human waste), have made standards of comfort and cleanliness much better over the last century.

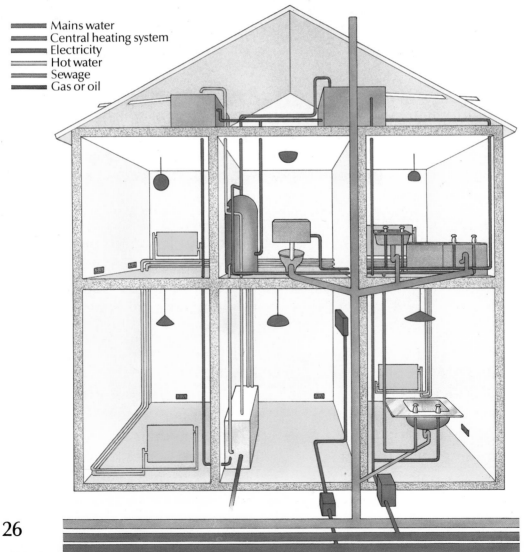

Mains water
Central heating system
Electricity
Hot water
Sewage
Gas or oil

Behind the walls and under the floorboards, plumbers put in a complicated system of copper or plastic pipes to carry water around the house. Water enters underground, through the mains pipe, which carries it up to a large cold water tank in the loft. From here, the water is fed to all the taps, toilets and hot water tanks. A smaller tank feeds the boiler and radiators of the central heating system.

Waste water from sinks, baths and toilets flows through a separate system of larger pipes, and is carried away underground to the mains sewage system.

Some of the pipes in the house have stopcocks to turn off the water supply. Manhole covers outside allow people to reach the drains.

The electrician lays two sets of cables around the house. One set is for lighting. The other carries a larger current (flow of electricity) to power sockets, for cookers, televisions and other gadgets. All the circuits are connected to the mains electricity supply, which enters the house through a meter and fuse box.

The hot water for the central heating system is fed around the house in pipes. This can be heated by gas or oil.

Left *Simplified diagram showing the services in a house.*

Right *A house in the USA which is heated by solar power, from the solar panels on the roof.*

The finishing touches

When the walls and roof have been built, there is still a lot of work to do before the house is finished.

Carpenters fit doors and windows into their frames, and build the wooden stairs. Moulded wooden or plaster **architrave** covers the joint where the walls meet the ceiling, and skirting boards are nailed around the bottom of the walls.

Above *An electrician wires a socket to the cables in the wall.*

Left *A glazier fixing a pane of glass in a window frame. The putty that has been run around the frame hardens and holds the glass in place.*

Left *Ceramic tiles are being positioned and stuck one at a time around the sink to prevent water or grease damaging the walls. When the tiles are dry, a thin layer of cement is pushed into the gaps between the tiles to keep the water out.*

Plasterers cover the rough inner walls and ceilings with a smooth layer of plaster, using a **float** for the final finish. Glaziers use putty to fit glass into the windows.

In their 'final fix', the plumbers connect the baths, sinks and taps to the water pipes. The electricians wire the light fittings and switches to the cables in the wall.

The central heating system is tested and telephone and television aerial cables are installed.

After this, the decorators can move in. In bathrooms and kitchens they cover the walls around baths and sinks with ceramic tiles to prevent water damage.

Decorators use different types of paint for different areas. Emulsion paint is ideal for inner walls and ceilings. It can be applied with a brush or a roller. Ceilings are often given a stippled (roughened) finish using a thicker paint.

Gloss paint is shiny and waterproof — excellent for use on outside woodwork, as well as doors and windows inside the house.

Exterior wall paint gives a tough finish which will last for many years.

Once the floor has been laid and carpets, tiles or vinyl sheeting put down, the house can finally be called a home. The new owners can move in.

Glossary

Adobe   Bricks of clay, dried in the sun.

Architect   Someone who designs buildings.

Architrave   Moulded length of wood, plaster or plastic, which covers the joint between the wall and ceiling.

Ashlar   Building stone cut into regular smooth-faced blocks.

Batten   Long narrow piece of timber used to support material on a roof.

Brace   Strengthening piece of iron or timber, which connects pairs of rafters.

Cladding   Coating or covering put over a structure.

Cob   A mixture of clay, straw and stones, used for building walls.

Course   A row of bricks or stones in a wall.

Eaves   The part of the roof that hangs over the outside wall.

Extrusion   Shaping a material by forcing it under pressure through a shaped hole — like toothpaste from a tube.

Flashing   Strip of metal or lead used to prevent flooding or leaking from a joint.

Float   Rectangular flat trowel for smoothing plaster.

Footings   The wide base of a wall, built under ground level, on the foundations.

Foundations   The strong base of a house, usually made by filling deep trenches with concrete.

Gable   Triangular upper part of a wall at the end of a sloping roof.

Girder construction   Building with large steel beams.

Hard-core   Stones, bricks or other materials used as a base for concrete floors.

Insulation   When a material is used to stop heat or sound passing through the walls, doors, or windows of a house.

Joist   Horizontal wooden or metal beam for supporting floors and roofs.

Lintel   Horizontal support above doors and windows to support a wall.

Mortar   Sand mixed with water and cement or lime, used to hold together the bricks or stones in a wall.

Pitched   Pitched roofs slope at an angle.

Plumbline   A lead weight on a string, used to check whether a wall is exactly upright, or whether it leans.

Rafters   Sloping timber supports for the roof, arranged in pairs.

Ridge-board   Beam of wood along the top of the roof where the rafters meet.

Rivetted   Metal plates fastened together by a bolt called a rivet.

Rubble   Stone in its rough, natural shape.

Shanty   A makeshift house, often built from waste materials.

Shuttering   Wood or metal moulds for shaping liquid concrete.

Spirit level   A straight bar of wood or metal, with an air bubble trapped in liquid, which shows if a wall is level.

Theodolite   A surveying instrument used to measure exact angles.

Wattle and daub   Mud or clay plastered on to a framework of woven sticks.

Books to read

Build a House by Heinz Kurth (Puffin, 1975).

Buildings and Building Sites by Eric Jones (Blandford, 1970).

How It's Built by Donald Clarke (Marshall Cavendish, 1979).

Homes by Margaret Crush (Franklin Watts, 1971).

Houses and Homes by Carol Bowyer (Usborne Publishing Ltd., 1978).

Houses and Homes by Carolyn Cocke (Macdonald Educational, 1976).

Houses and Homes by Heinz Kurth (World's Work Ltd., 1980).

Looking at Houses by Audrey Gee (Batsford, 1983).

Skyscrapers (Macdonald First Library, 1972).

Picture Acknowledgements

The author and publishers would like to thank the following for allowing their illustrations to be reproduced in this book: Bryan and Cherry Alexander 10; Building Research Station (Department of the Environment) 11 (left); Cement and Concrete Association 21 (top and bottom); Bruce Coleman 7 (top); Chris Fairclough 28 (left and right), 30; Andy Hasson 11 (right); The Hutchison Library 15 (top), 23 (top); Christine Osborne 8, 9 (bottom); Graham Rickard 13 (bottom left), 20, 23 (bottom); Sefton 17 (bottom); Topham 5 (bottom), 7 (bottom), 13 (top right); ZEFA *Cover*, 4, 5 (top), 12, 14, 15 (bottom), 16, 17, (top), 18 (top), 19 (top), 25, 27; Laura Zito 9 (top). All other pictures from the Wayland Picture Library.

Index